Bible reflections
for older people

BRF

The Bible Reading Fellowship
15 The Chambers, Vineyard
Abingdon OX14 3FE
brf.org.uk

The Bible Reading Fellowship (BRF) is a Registered Charity (233280)

ISBN 978 0 85746 908 3

Acknowledgements
Scripture quotations marked with the following acronyms are taken from the version shown. Where no acronym is given, the quotation is taken from the same version as the headline reference. **NIV** or **NIV 1984**: The Holy Bible, New International Version (Anglicised edition) copyright © 1979, 1984, 2011 by Biblica. Used by permission of Hodder & Stoughton Publishers, a Hachette UK company. All rights reserved. 'NIV' is a registered trademark of Biblica. UK trademark number 1448790. **NLT**: The Holy Bible, New Living Translation, copyright © 1996, 2004, 2007, 2013. Used by permission of Tyndale House Publishers, Inc., Carol Stream, Illinois 60188. All rights reserved. **MSG**: *The Message*, copyright © 1993, 1994, 1995, 1996, 2000, 2001, 2002 by Eugene H. Peterson. Used by permission of NavPress. All rights reserved. Represented by Tyndale House Publishers, Inc.

Photograph of Paul Canon Harris © Clare Park 2014. Used with permission.

Poems on pages 33–34 © Robert (Bob) G.P. Weighton from *Diverse Verses* (2018). Used with permission.

Every effort has been made to trace and contact copyright owners for material used in this resource. We apologise for any inadvertent omissions or errors, and would ask those concerned to contact us so that full acknowledgement can be made in the future.

A catalogue record for this book is available from the British Library

Printed and bound in the UK by Zenith Media NP4 0DQ

Contents

About the writers

Paul Canon Harris is a poet, writer and broadcaster based in Bournemouth. His published work includes two poetry collections, a novel and non-fiction works on spirituality and leadership. He is married to Cathy, a speech therapist, and they have four sons, ten grandchildren and a dog called Hope.

Lin Ball's career as a wordsmith began in news journalism, and interviewing people is still one of her favourite things. Over the years as an editor and writer, she's brought to the shelves over 200 books, mainly Bible resources for Scripture Union, but also a number of life stories and titles in areas such as disability.

Ro Willoughby has been writing and editing Christian resources for many years. She has recently been licensed as a lay minister at St Chad's Woodseats in Sheffield, where she is engaged in ministry with people of all ages. It is a great joy that she now lives close to her children and grandchildren.

Margot and Martin Hodson: Margot is Director of Theology and Education for the John Ray Initiative (JRI), an organisation connecting environment, science and Christianity, and an Anglican minister in the Oxford Diocese. Martin is a plant scientist and environmental biologist. He is Operations Director for JRI. The Hodsons have been published widely and have written several books including *A Christian Guide to Environmental Issues* (BRF, 2015). For more about the Hodsons, see their website, **hodsons.org**.

From the Editor

Welcome to this new collection of Bible reflections.

I rang Bob Weighton at 11.30 one morning, a week before his 111th birthday. No, that's not a misprint. 'Is this a good time, Bob?' I asked. 'Well, I am just cooking my lunch,' he replied.

I left him to his cooking and called back later to record the interview that appears in part in this issue of *Bible Reflections for Older People* and in full on the Anna Chaplaincy website: **annachaplaincy.org.uk/ bob-weighton**.

It was a remarkable conversation, ranging from the outbreak of World War I, when Bob was six years old, through the Great Depression and the Wall Street Crash, on to World War II and the Cold War, all the way through to Brexit, terrorism and the resurgence of far-right parties all over Europe. The number of centenarians, at least in countries with good nutrition and medical care, is growing every decade, but Bob is a 'super-centenarian'.

What made our conversation so compelling was his full and vivid recall of all the history he had lived through, and of its impact on his own life, the lives of his family, friends and colleagues, and on his enduring faith.

'If anything,' he says, 'I've become even more devoted to the peace movement as the years have gone on – who couldn't be? Every Christian should be.'

God bless you

Using these reflections

Perhaps you have always had a special daily time for reading the Bible and praying. But now, as you grow older, you are finding it more difficult to keep to a regular pattern or find it hard to concentrate. Or maybe you've never done this before. Whatever your situation, these Bible reflections aim to help you take a few moments to read God's word and pray, whenever you have time or feel that would be helpful.

When to read them

You may find it helpful to use these Bible reflections in the morning or last thing at night, or any time during the day. There are 40 daily reflections here, grouped around four themes. Each one includes some verses from the Bible, a reflection to help you in your own thinking about God, and a prayer suggestion. The reflections aren't dated, so it doesn't matter if you don't want to read every day. The Bible verses are printed, but if you'd like to read from your own Bible that's fine too.

How to read them

- **Take time** to quieten yourself, becoming aware of God's presence, asking him to speak to you through the Bible and the reflection.

- **Read** the Bible verses and the reflection:
  - What do you especially like or find helpful in these verses?
  - What might God be saying to you through this reading?
  - Is there something to pray about or thank God for?

- **Pray**. Each reflection includes a prayer suggestion. You might like to pray for yourself or take the opportunity to think about and pray for others.

The runaways

Paul Canon Harris

Running away is sometimes associated with cowardice, but it can also be an act of common sense, as when fleeing danger. In a military context, it can be a response to a command to retreat in order to regroup. The Bible records instances of people running away for all sorts of reasons.

My uncle was evacuated during World War II. To escape the Blitz, he was one of thousands of youngsters bizarrely sent to the south coast, which was a prime location for invading forces. He was an unhappy twelve-year-old in Hove. He asked his father to send his bike by train. As soon as it arrived at the station, he jumped on it and cycled back to London. Arriving exhausted late at night, he was not sent back.

The epistles include advice to stand and resist the evil one (James 4:7) but also to flee temptation (2 Timothy 2:22). It is important in life to know whether you are running from something or running towards something, and to know when to stand firm and when to flee. The characters in these meditations faced challenges and trials which made them run, and yet in the end they experienced God as sovereign in their lives. Life on the run is no fun: running into the arms of our loving heavenly Father is wonderful.

Genesis 27:42–44 (NIV 1984)

A cheating brother flees

When Rebekah was told what her older son Esau had said, she sent for her younger son Jacob and said to him, 'Your brother Esau is consoling himself with the thought of killing you. Now then, my son, do what I say: Flee at once to my brother Laban in Haran. Stay there until your brother's fury subsides.'

My wife Cathy and I raised four sons, who now appear to be relatively responsible adults. This still surprises us somewhat. Looking back, the air in our house seemed thick with testosterone. They were very competitive; there were frequent accusations of cheating in board games. 'Boys, stop fighting – go into separate rooms till you have calmed down!' was our regular response.

In families as in battle, a strategic retreat gives people space to calm down and allows others to get out of range. Jacob spent much of his early life on the run – from family, from enemies, even from God – largely because of fear and guilt. His mother urged him to flee his enraged brother Esau, whom he had tricked. Maturity brought stability and peace as he got in step with God's plan for his life. That is not an automatic process. By nature, I like to confront issues as soon as possible. Even though I am older now, I have to remember that backing off is sometimes the better thing to do.

■ PRAYER
Father God, I pray for families and households where sibling rivalry, jealousy and resentment is driving people apart. Amen

Genesis 39:6b–7a, 11–12 (NIV)

Fleeing temptation

Joseph was well-built and handsome, and after a while his master's wife took notice of Joseph… One day he went into the house to attend to his duties, and none of the household servants was inside. She caught him by his cloak and said, 'Come to bed with me!' But he left his cloak in her hand and ran out of the house.

Joseph is an example of someone who knew the importance of fleeing temptation. As a young man, I was given advice about the power of sexual attraction. A student worker warned me, 'If you don't want to finish up in Boston, don't get on the Boston train.' Through all my years as a vicar I lost count of the times people who messed up their relationships through infidelity said, 'We didn't intend to do it – one thing led to another.' That's the Boston train.

God intended to use Joseph in his purposes for his people. Joseph's ability to recognise temptation and to flee it showed necessary quality of character.

This dynamic applies as much to gossip or greed as it does to sexual temptation. There is usually a point when we can choose to escape. Purity and holiness are not primarily things God wants *from* us so much as things he wants *for* us – whatever our age.

■ PRAYER

Loving God, you know my inner thoughts, my hopes and desires: help me to choose purity. I pray for those struggling with temptation of any sort. Amen

Exodus 2:11b–12, 15a (NIV 1984)

Blood on his hands

Moses... saw an Egyptian beating a Hebrew, one of his own people. Glancing this way and that and seeing no-one, he killed the Egyptian and hid him in the sand... When Pharaoh heard of this, he tried to kill Moses, but Moses fled from Pharaoh and went to live in Midian.

Who would want to be a member of the royal family or a politician? Their every move is scrutinised by the media and people are quick to pillory them for the slightest indiscretion, though certainly some bring trouble on themselves. That was true in Moses' case.

Brought up in the royal palace, as if a prince of Egypt, people still knew that Moses was from the enslaved Jewish people. One day, his loyalties were sorely tested. Intervening impulsively, he killed an Egyptian and tried to cover up his crime. He thought he had got away with it, but he soon discovered there were witnesses to his actions and he had to flee to yet another foreign land, a displaced person with a guilty secret. He escaped punishment, but he couldn't escape the truth of what he had done.

Changing our location does not necessarily change our inner landscape. Only facing up to what we have done and seeking God's forgiveness can do that.

■ **PRAYER**
Jesus, liberator of captives, I pray for all who are captive to regret and who struggle to find forgiveness. Amen

1 Samuel 19:11–12 (NIV)

Fleeing a jealous king

Saul sent men to David's house to watch it and to kill him in the morning. But Michal, David's wife, warned him, 'If you don't run for your life tonight, tomorrow you'll be killed.' So Michal let David down through a window, and he fled and escaped.

King Saul was jealous of David. Jealousy usually has a corrosive effect; in this story, it had damaged Saul and David's relationship irreparably so that David was in real and present danger. Saul had previously tried to kill David by throwing a spear at him, and his escape was a matter of life and death. Michal, his wife, recognised this and urged him to flee. Wisely, he took her advice.

Hopefully, very few of us will ever face such a murderous threat, but no one is immune from the dangers of jealousy and its close relation, envy. While jealousy is the fear that something we have will be taken away by someone else, envy is coveting what someone else has. Both can give rise to inner battles; both corrode friendship and contentment; and we should do all we can to flee them both.

I have also come to realise that I can unwittingly be a cause of jealousy and envy. If I am insensitive when talking about some of the blessings in my life – my grandchildren, for example – I can trigger difficult emotions in other people. That is certainly never my intention, but it's something I need to be aware of and take steps to avoid.

■ PRAYER

God of contentment and peace, please help those who struggle with jealousy and envy. Keep me sensitive to other people's situations. Amen

1 Kings 19:3–4 (NIV 1984)

Fear and burnout

Elijah was afraid and ran for his life. When he came to Beersheba in Judah, he left his servant there, while he himself went a day's journey into the desert. He came to a broom tree, sat down under it and prayed that he might die. 'I have had enough, Lord,' he said. 'Take my life; I am no better than my ancestors.'

Elijah was another of God's servants who had to flee from an angry king. Having seen God display his awesome power to the pagan prophets, Elijah came back to earth with a bump. He was burned out physically, emotionally and spiritually. Displaying the classic symptoms of depression, he'd had enough and yearned to escape. His perspective was skewed, he didn't want company or help and he wished God would end his life.

Eventually, he lay down under a tree and fell asleep. Over the next few days, God refreshed and restored him – meeting his physical need for sleep and food before recommissioning him.

Over-busy people often keep running, partly out of habit and partly from fear of losing significance or position. That is why retirement can be such a hard adjustment and people struggle to stop running, but it's a dangerous strategy. I recently began a poem with these words: 'If I don't unwind, I will unravel, if I don't slow up, I will grind to a halt.'

■ **PRAYER**

God, the great restorer, draw close to those caught between feeling they cannot go on and feeling they cannot stop running. Amen

Jonah 1:1–3 (NIV, abridged)

Fleeing God's calling

The word of the Lord came to Jonah… 'Go to the great city of Nineveh and preach against it…' But Jonah ran away from the Lord and headed for Tarshish. He went down to Joppa, where he found a ship bound for that port. After paying the fare, he went aboard and sailed for Tarshish to flee from the Lord.

If Jonah was one of the Mister Men in the famous children's books and cartoons, it would be hard to decide whether he should be Mr Timid, Mr Naughty or Mr Angry. He was frightened and reluctant to obey God's call. I can relate to that.

Later, after his fishy adventure and having preached in Nineveh, Jonah became angry when God showed compassion on the city. What a mixed-up preacher.

In this stage of my life, I might think that God is unlikely to send me to preach in a foreign city, though I have done that in the past. Then I remind myself that there is no early retirement in God's service. He may well call me to do something unexpected or to speak a message of his love to someone, and even now, after all these years, I may initially struggle to obey. The lesson of Jonah is that reluctant disciples can run but they can't hide. Obedience sooner rather than later is better for all concerned.

■ PRAYER

God, thank you that you understand my timidity. Help me to overcome my fears so that I can serve you and those around me. Amen

Matthew 2:13–14 (NIV)

Fleeing in obedience

When [the Magi] had gone, an angel of the Lord appeared to Joseph in a dream. 'Get up,' he said, 'take the child and his mother and escape to Egypt. Stay there until I tell you, for Herod is going to search for the child to kill him.' So he got up, took the child and his mother during the night and left for Egypt.

Human history is littered with accounts of people having to flee to escape enemies intent on killing them. The Son of God was a genuine refugee. Staying put was not a choice for the family; it was a case of leave or die. During his earthly ministry, Jesus faced the threat of death, not least when he had to slip away from an angry home-town crowd intent on throwing him over a cliff.

Knowing when to run and when to stand your ground in life requires great wisdom. It is important to try to stay attuned to God's prompting – however it comes. He is our protector and has our times in his hands, just as he had a definite plan and timescale for his Son's life.

The plight of refugees is a contemporary and contentious issue. Repressive governments threaten to wipe out minorities. Death is a real and present danger in war-torn regions. As it was for Jesus' family, fleeing is sometimes the only option, no matter how perilous the journey.

■ PRAYER

Almighty God, please be with refugees in danger in our world today, and with those who seek to help and protect them. Amen

John 4:28–29 (NIV 1984)

Fleeing in eagerness

Then leaving her water jar, the woman went back to the town and said to the people, 'Come, see a man who told me everything I ever did. Could this be the Christ?'

I love the story of Jesus' encounter with the woman at the well of Samaria. Collecting water alone in the heat of the day suggests that she was something of an outcast her in own community. She certainly had a colourful past and possibly guilty secrets. When Jesus revealed that he knew all about her, the exchange between the two of them changed. The woman started to engage with Jesus on a spiritual level. Jesus declared himself to be the Christ.

The previously secretive woman now rushed back to the town to invite her neighbours and strangers to come and meet Jesus. Many would run a mile from someone who knew all about them – but not in this case. This woman was so eager that she even left her heavy stone water pot by the well, along with the sense of shame that had weighed so heavily on her.

God's full knowledge of us, warts and all, is not something to be frightened of or to flee from. We are liberated by his acceptance and forgiveness; we no longer need to pretend nor to run.

■ PRAYER
God, the keeper of secrets, thank you for your unconditional love and acceptance. I pray today for any known to me who are weighed down by guilt or shame. Amen

Mark 14:51–52 (NIV)

Fleeing naked

A young man, wearing nothing but a linen garment, was following Jesus. When they seized him, he fled naked, leaving his garment behind.

I often wonder if I will ever develop a grown-up sense of humour. As a child in Sunday school, the account of a young man (probably John Mark) running away, leaving his robe behind him, when Jesus was arrested was one of my favourite Bible stories. 'Please, can we act it out?' There was something heroic about such a narrow – and, to the mind of a nine-year-old boy – ridiculously rude escape. I still – and please don't judge me too harshly for this – cheer streakers at sports events. There is something wonderfully anarchic about them.

John Mark was not a deserter. A young man, his whole life before him, he was running away to fight another day. It was important for him to stay free and become all that God wanted him to be. He wrote Mark's gospel; he accompanied Paul and Barnabas on missionary journeys; and he had the gift of comforting others.

Mark ran away instinctively, out of fear, not cowardice. His instinct was right. Even if in the past we have fled situations in fear, it is encouraging to see how, down the line, God can turn that flight to his purpose.

■ **PRAYER**

God, the great rescuer, thank you for my escapes in life. Be close to those today who are fleeing danger. Protect them for what their futures hold. Amen

John 21:2–3a (NIV)

Fleeing disappointment

Simon Peter, Thomas (called Didymus), Nathanael from Cana in Galilee, the sons of Zebedee, and two other disciples were together. 'I'm going out to fish,' Simon Peter told them, and they said, 'We'll go with you.'

There has been much debate over the years about whether in this passage Peter was, in common parlance, 'doing a runner' and calling it a day as a disciple. Returning to his roots, to what he knew, namely fishing, made sense and was not altogether unreasonable. Perhaps it was a classic response to grief. His dearest friend Jesus had died. Peter was wracked with guilt due to his denial and was trying to make sense of Jesus' amazing resurrection appearances. He had to do something.

Whatever was behind his decision to go fishing, he was carrying pain and emotional baggage. He did not realise it then, but God still intended him to play a key role in spreading the good news of the risen Christ. It would take a beach-side breakfast and a restorative 'clear the air' walk with Jesus to get him right.

I have been disappointed by and with others in life, but by far my greatest disappointments have been with myself, for the times in my life that have been a denial of God's calling on my life. Peter's experience reminds me that Jesus comes after the runaways and draws them back into his loving purpose.

■ **PRAYER**
Jesus, seeker of runaways, please draw close to any who feel they have failed you and are close to giving up. Amen

Coming home

Lin Ball

'Aah… that feels good!' Home after an evening out, my husband and I slip out of our glad rags and into our old fleece dressing gowns.

What does 'home' mean to you? It's such an evocative word. At best, it's the place where you find light in the darkness. I hope your home is a place of comfort, security, sanctuary… a place where you can be yourself in shabby slippers. But even if it isn't physically those things, it can be spiritually.

On the Bristol council estate where I grew up, an elderly woman and her unmarried son solemnly passed our gate each Sunday morning en route to church, dressed soberly in black, clutching big Bibles. They provoked predictable mockery from my father. In our home, the name of Jesus was only a swear word.

At 18, at a very low point, I encountered God and my life was transformed. When I married at 20, I determined that our home – then two rented rooms with a shared toilet downstairs – would be a place where God and his word were respected and loved.

I hope these notes help you look at your home with fresh and grateful eyes.

Deuteronomy 11:18–20 (NLT, abridged)

God in our home

Commit yourselves wholeheartedly to these words of mine…
Teach them to your children. Talk about them when you are at
home… when you are going to bed and when you are getting up.
Write them on the doorposts of your house and on your gates.

This description of a home in Deuteronomy is enlightening and challenging. The most prominent feature is the respect and love given to the word of God. It's physically evident everywhere. It pervades the atmosphere. It's the easy topic of conversation from morning to night.

Today, we're unlikely to have Bible verses actually on our person in the way Jewish men wore phylacteries – small leather boxes containing texts on vellum as reminders to keep God's laws – although we might have Bible verses on posters or fridge magnets.

Modelling this passage, home is the place where we are most 'present' to God – in our hearts, minds and conversations. It's where we talk about him and his love as naturally as talking about the weather.

I'm glad that the scene I remember most from our first home – those two rented rooms – is sitting in the bay window reading my New Testament before heading off to work. Today, now both retired, my husband and I open the Bible at the kitchen table after breakfast to read and pray together.

■ **PRAYER**

Pray for members of your family, your church family or your neigh-
bours, who visit you where you live. How do you and your home
communicate to them your love of God and God's word?

Acts 2:44, 46–47a (NLT)

Open house

And all the believers met together in one place and shared everything they had… They worshipped together at the Temple each day, met in homes for the Lord's Supper, and shared their meals with great joy and generosity – all the while praising God and enjoying the goodwill of all the people.

What an incredibly joyful picture of the church family is conveyed in these few sentences. Hospitality, generosity, meeting each other's needs – all these are evident within the context of vibrant and all-encompassing worship of God. And note that, while the temple is used, the experiences of the believers spill over naturally into ordinary homes.

The Bible doesn't recognise 'Sunday-only Christians': keeping faith in a box, bringing it out once a week, but on Monday mornings being indistinguishable from anyone else, with work and home life falling into step with the values of the world. Love for God informs and directs all we are, seven days a week.

However humble our home, however restricted our circumstances, we can be generous and hospitable. Jesus said that even a cup of water shared in his name was something he would reward (Matthew 10:42). This kind of faith is wonderfully contagious.

■ PRAYER

Express your gratitude to God for the roof over your head, the food in your cupboard. Ask him how your thankfulness can be communicated to others. Who could you invite in for a cup of coffee this week?

John 14:21, 23b (NIV)

Safe house

'Whoever has my commands and keeps them is the one who loves me. The one who loves me will be loved by my Father, and I too will love them and show myself to them… and we will come to them and make our home with them.'

The prodigal son (Luke 15:11–20) is one of the best-loved stories that Jesus told. Salvation – finding faith in Jesus – is a homecoming. As 'Amazing Grace' puts it: 'I once was lost, but now am found.' Life apart from our creator is a deeply uncomfortable 'lostness'. When we find him – or allow him to find us – there is a sense of belonging, of coming home, that we may never have experienced before.

A friend had a vision in which she saw Jesus and his Father moving around doing small domestic tasks in her kitchen. As she watched them, astonished, from her open-plan lounge, they came to her, sat on the floor and lovingly washed her feet. Writing about the experience, she says, 'We remain together, content, in companionship. There is no need to leave this place. The house is mine, but now his. It is a safe house, where I am loved.'*

Jesus and the Father want to make their home with us, his followers… a safe house, where we are loved.

■ PRAYER

Make your home with me, Lord Jesus. I want my life to be so open to you and your love that we are as close as it's possible to be. Amen

* Peppy Ulyett, *The Chronicles of the Box* (Malcolm Down Publishing, 2017)

John 10:14–16 (NIV, abridged)

In his flock

*'I am the good shepherd; I know my sheep and my sheep know me…
and I lay down my life for the sheep. I have other sheep that are not
of this sheepfold… They too will listen to my voice, and there shall be
one flock and one shepherd.'*

I've always loved to travel. But there's something especially lovely
about returning after a time away, putting the key in the lock and
breathing in the sanctuary of the place I call home.

Though it's over-sentimental, many of us would agree with John
Howard Payne's song 'Home Sweet Home', from his 1822 opera
Clari, or the Maid of Milan: 'Mid pleasures and palaces though we
may roam,/Be it ever so humble, there's no place like home.'

That sense of being 'at home' finds resonance in this Bible passage.
To know Jesus and to be known by him, to recognise his voice…
there is so much comfort in that familiarity. Of course, the danger is
that 'familiarity breeds contempt'. But as we daily remind ourselves
of all that the good shepherd endured on the cross so that we could
be one of his much-loved flock, that possibility recedes.

■ **PRAYER**

*'One flock and one shepherd' (v. 16). Thank God for drawing you into
the flock of Christ. Pray for a sense of unity among believers in Jesus.
Name others before him who need to feel 'at home' with God.*

Jeremiah 50:6 (MSG)

Homeless

'My people were lost sheep. Their shepherds led them astray. They abandoned them in the mountains where they wandered aimless through the hills. They lost track of home, couldn't remember where they came from.'

The charity Shelter put the 2017 figure for the whole of the UK's homeless at 300,000. Despite the relative affluence of the nation, rough sleeping is on the increase.

The Bible shows us a God who is concerned about the physical well-being of people, as well as passionate about their spiritual state. Here in Jeremiah, the 'lostness' of people without God is compared to desperate homelessness. According to the prophet, people are in that situation because they've been led astray, in the way that sheep with an uncaring shepherd wander off the path. Abandoned, aimless, they lose sight of shelter. Thus exposed, they are vulnerable to attacks of the enemy, like the rough sleepers who are often the victims of robbery and violence in the hidden alleys of our big cities and run-down seaside towns.

Just as salvation is a kind of homecoming, straying from Jesus is a kind of homelessness, whether self-imposed or the result of poor leadership. We will stay on the right path if we keep listening to him.

■ PRAYER

Ask Jesus, the good shepherd, to keep you close. Pray for any you know who are physically homeless; and then for any you know who are spiritually homeless. May they hear the voice of Jesus calling them home, and find safety.

Mark 10:29 (MSG)

Holding home lightly

Jesus said, 'Mark my words, no one who sacrifices house, brothers, sisters, mother, father, children, land – whatever – because of me and the Message will lose out.'

The first home we had a mortgage on was a two-up, two-down Victorian terraced house in an Oxfordshire village. We loved that little home. We painstakingly renovated the wooden sash windows; we uncovered the original tiling in the hallway; we painted the cast-iron fireplaces. We divided the larger bedroom so that our two children could have their own rooms for the first time.

And then came the call to Christian work in Asia.

For the next ten years, we lived in different rented flats, first in Hong Kong and then in Singapore, as my husband joined United Bible Societies as a consultant for Bible production across Asia.

Following Jesus can sometimes mean sacrificing your bricks-and-mortar home and being far from family and friends. Would we rather have stayed home? No. We would have missed out on the enriching, faith-building experience of finding our true home in God's will, and of getting to know new brothers and sisters in Christ from many nations.

Though God may bless you with a wonderful home, remember to hold it lightly.

■ PRAYER
Thank God for those who are willing to leave home and family to share the good news of Jesus. Ask God to make you willing to be available to him whenever he calls.

Isaiah 32:17–18 (NIV)

Finding ourselves

The fruit of that righteousness will be peace; its effect will be quietness and confidence for ever. My people will live in peaceful dwelling-places, in secure homes, in undisturbed places of rest.

'The ache for home lives in all of us… the safe place where we can go as we are and not be questioned.' So wrote the acclaimed American writer Maya Angelou in her autobiographical *All God's Children Need Traveling Shoes*. She struggled with her roots, and with the fact that her Ghanaian ancestors were sold into slavery. Returning to Africa in the 1960s, she hoped to find 'home' and to find herself.

We all, to some extent, recognise that search for true identity. I've lived for the past ten years in a pretty market town in the East Midlands. I feel at home here. But I've also lived in a flat above an empty shop in a rundown area of Bristol; on the fifteenth floor of a block overlooking the heat-hazed Tolo Harbour in Hong Kong; and across the road from the Botanic Gardens in clean and green Singapore. I can truly say that whenever I feel at home with God, at peace with him, then I have felt content in my situation, wherever I am. Yes, it's true: 'home is where the heart is'.

■ PRAYER

Father God, my desire is for a peaceful, secure home, an undisturbed place of rest. May I not only experience that physically but find that in knowing you and being loved by you. Amen

Psalm 84:1, 3–5 (NIV, abridged)

Set on pilgrimage

How lovely is your dwelling-place, Lord Almighty!… Even the sparrow has found a home, and the swallow a nest for herself, where she may have her young – a place near your altar, Lord Almighty, my King and my God. Blessed are those who dwell in your house… Blessed are those whose strength is in you, whose hearts are set on pilgrimage.

Many of us have a 'nesting instinct', a longing to settle down and make a home, even if we live in just one room. The Christian has to balance this with the calling to be a pilgrim, whether that's physical or spiritual in its outworking. In this psalm, the two ideas exist side by side, with no contradiction.

A song that has been sung by believers as a comfort during times of hardship or dislocation is 'This world is not my home; I'm just a-passin' through'. We are promised an eternal home that will more than recompense us for difficulties in this world. That's why we must counter our longing for an earthly home with a dedication to moving on as needed, to pilgrimage with God. As Jesus said, 'My Father's house has many rooms; if that were not so, would I have told you that I am going there to prepare a place for you?' (John 14:2).

■ PRAYER

Praise God if you have found a safe place to call home in this world. Thank him that even if you have not, the ache for home will find its satisfaction in the next world.

Revelation 21:3–4a (NLT)

Ultimate homecoming

I heard a loud shout from the throne, saying, 'Look, God's home is now among his people! He will live with them, and they will be his people. God himself will be with them. He will wipe every tear from their eyes, and there will be no more death or sorrow or crying or pain.'

During a time of painful disappointment about my career, God felt remote for long months. I felt on the verge of clinical depression, something I had known in my teens before becoming a Christian. I felt a failure that I should experience this as a believer. Where was my joy?

It's all too easy to rely on what we feel rather than what we know. I constantly reminded myself of God's promise never to leave me (Hebrews 13:5). I was helped by thinking through the 'now but not yet' of God's kingdom. What joy to read of God wiping the tears from our eyes, of the banishing of pain and death. We must trust that day will come, even though we live in the 'not yet' days. Our confidence is in the fact, not the feeling.

See how that time is described (v. 3). The expression of our forever union with him is described as the ultimate homecoming. Wonderful!

■ **PRAYER**

Tell your Father how you feel that one day you will be at home with him among his people. Then unite that feeling with a statement of confident faith: may it be so. Amen

Psalm 119:173–176 (MSG, abridged)

Letters from home

I'm homesick, God, for your salvation… Invigorate my soul so I can praise you well, use your decrees to put iron in my soul. And should I wander off like a lost sheep – seek me! I'll recognise the sound of your voice.

As I write these notes, my daughter is on a five-week research trip to South America. She is in Bogota, Columbia, and she is sick. The 'pings' of her daily WhatsApp texts reassure me, though at times I lie awake at night in some anxiety that she is safe. It's hard to be away from home when you feel unwell.

This psalm, beautifully realised by Eugene Peterson in *The Message* paraphrase, is a prayer about a specific kind of homesickness – a yearning for God's salvation. The writer wants to be rescued and brought home like a lost sheep on the good shepherd's shoulders (Luke 15:5).

The early church leader Augustine said, 'The Holy Scriptures are our letters from home.' I hope my texts to my daughter bring her the reminder she may need, when she is feeling low, that she is loved and precious.

And whenever I'm longing for the things of God, or feel far away or unhappy, I can open his letters to find reassurance, hope, renewal – and the promise of home.

■ **PRAYER**

Father, help me to remember, whenever I need reassurance, that I have 'letters from home'. Amen

The Gift of Years

 Debbie Thrower is the Pioneer of BRF's Anna Chaplaincy for Older People ministry, offering spiritual care to older people, and is widely involved in training and advocacy.

Visit **annachaplaincy.org.uk** to find out more.

Debbie writes…

Welcome! How well do you know yourself, and your ageing self in particular? 'Know thyself,' urged the Ancient Greeks. The philosopher, Socrates, wrote, 'The unexamined life is not worth living.' But as we grow older, we don't always grow wiser as a matter of course. We, possibly, need some help.

A theme common to many of our reflections is that of self-awareness. I've noticed as I get older how my capacity for fooling myself is as strong as ever; witness my surprise when I catch sight of myself in a mirror and the person I feel on the inside doesn't match the face others see.

All our current reflections are written by people who've wrestled with similar feelings of dissonance. How to resolve the incongruity of who we are, and what we might like to be as the years roll by, is a topic our writers address in a variety of ways within these pages. Trying to be the best version of 'me' that I can be is, clearly, a lifetime's occupation.

I hope you'll be helped in this task by reflecting alongside these gifted writers, who are 'people like us', and discerning what it is to grow old faithfully and gracefully.

My best wishes

Meet Bob Weighton

 Bob Weighton was born on 29 March 1908 and, as this edition of *Bible Reflections for Older People* goes to print, he is Britain's oldest man. A 'super-centenarian', Bob was born and brought up in Hull in Yorkshire and trained as a marine engineer. Things didn't quite work out as planned, but he's had a rich and varied international life with a focus on peace-making and the worldwide church. His wife died in 1995 and he lost one of his sons in 2014. He has two surviving children, ten grandchildren and at the last count, 25 great-grandchildren. Faith has been an enduring strand in his life and he has always written poetry. A good friend of Anna Chaplaincy founder Debbie Thrower, Bob was instrumental in her early work with older people in Alton, Hampshire. He talked to *Bible Reflections for Older People* Editor, Eley McAinsh, just before his 111th birthday, about how his poetry fitted with his work as a marine engineer. He says:

Engineers are looked upon as being ignorant of everything but engineering and assumed to go around in a boiler suit with an oil can in one hand and a big spanner in the other. So there's a prejudice about engineers in the world of the arts, but it's quite ridiculous. Leonardo da Vinci was certainly an engineer as well as a poet and artist.

You were a teacher in a mission school in Taiwan as a young man – what took you there?

You never know exactly why you do things, but there were quite a few contributory causes which led me to volunteer to go abroad as a missionary. One big factor was that when I graduated, and after my apprenticeship, the Great Depression came along. The Wall Street Crash in 1929 hit the United States and the engineering firm that I did my apprenticeship with got less and less busy as time went on.

I thought of lecturing in a technical college and I did apply for those roles, but at the same time, alongside my job search, I had a very strong Christian faith and as a student in university I came into contact with the Student Christian Movement. It still exists, but not in the way that it did in my day, when leading theologians would come and give a series of lectures at the annual Swanwick conference. I went three years in succession. There were so many people there that the men were all encamped in marquees in the grounds. They were great fun and the emphasis was very much on the world church, and that was another factor to stimulate the idea of going abroad myself.

When I did write to find out what I could do, they said, 'Oh, we want an English teacher in Taiwan.' So I went up to Selly Oak to train and after the course I steamed out to Taiwan, where I stayed until the outbreak of World War II, except for an interlude in Japan, where I went for language study because at that time Taiwan was a colony of the Japanese Empire and Japanese was the official language.

You said in another interview, 'I've seen the world fall apart twice.' How did that experience affect you?

I don't know what I would be without those experiences. Of course, I was only a young child – six years of age – when World War I broke out, and my world was the world of a child of six. I saw soldiers on the streets, and the young men who came to say goodbye to my mother and father and all they talked about was 'going to France'. I had no idea what France was then, but of course most of them didn't come back and by the age of ten, when the war ended, I'd begun to realise.

After the war, when I was in my teens and at college, 'world peace' was a prime conviction of most young people of my age. We were all naive enough to think that we would be different; ours would be the generation that was going to see world peace, but of course it didn't happen that way.

After all you have seen, and given the state we seem to be in now, are you hopeful for the world, hopeful for the future?

I'm hopeful because I believe in the ultimate victory of peace. It's not a naive hope. I hope that there are enough of us who will stand up against those who hate and blame others on the basis of race, sex, nationality or anything else. We have to fight this on all sorts of different fronts in society, and especially in all those places where far-right parties are on the rise. As I say, I'm hopeful because I believe in the ultimate victory of peace, but the outlook is not very bright at the moment. If anything, I've become even more devoted to the peace movement as the years have gone on – who couldn't be? Every Christian should be.

Easter, 1941

You knew, that night, what things would come to pass
Before the dawn. You saw the traitor's hand.
You watched the unrelenting moments pass
Through that last supper with the little band;
So weak, not grasping yet the day, the hour,
So quick to boast, and yet how soon to flee
Before the breaking storm. What mortal power
Held your voice steady then, when you could see
The garden's darkness and those men asleep
Whilst you fought out that last fierce fight with sin,
The Judgement Hall, the angry mob, the steep
Road to a rock? What spirit reigned within
That heart of yours, lent quiet to your eyes
And grace to hands which lifted up the bread
And blessed it, whilst the darkening Syrian skies
Grew heavy with the pressing shades of dread?
Oh Jesus, soul of courage, spirit's food,
Nerve my faint heart with thine own fortitude.

Robert (Bob) G.P. Weighton. Hartford, Conn. 1941

Memories

Memories are like pearls
Threaded on the cord of Time.
And there are none I treasure more
Than those whose clear
Translucent depths
Reflect as yesterday those hours,
Plucked from all cares and busyness,
When we could share
Music, a woodland walk,
Or simply talk
Over a meal; or where
You could curl up in a chair
At home.
Rosie, for all of these,
I thank you.

Morning

And I must off and on my way,
For God is abroad in the world today!

Barrow-on-Humber, 1927

From *Diverse Verses* by Robert (Bob) G.P. Weighton, 2018. Used with kind permission.

Treasure, hidden in a field

Extract from *Turned by Divine Love*
by John Stroyan

Turned by
Divine Love
Starting again with God and with others
JOHN STROYAN

There is something important... about the hiddenness of the kingdom of God: something about the tiny, almost invisible, mustard seed relative to the huge and majestic cedar of Lebanon. There is something about the way God works, so often unseen or unnoticed, beneath the radar of public news, away from the limelight of media or social media. The kingdom of God, Jesus says, is like treasure hidden in a field. I remember well walking on the island of Mull and a long way from any path, coming across some of the most beautiful lilies I have ever seen growing entirely away from the gaze and appreciation of humanity. But, I wondered, was the fact that their beauty would hardly ever be seen by people important? Apparently not to God, I thought...

I think... of a deeply saintly woman, Mabel, unknown to almost everybody, who was housebound, living high up in a tower block of flats in an inner-city parish in which I served. She, in her great humility and prayerfulness, radiated the love of Christ. When I and other clergy met with her, we knew we were on holy ground. On her little balcony, she had stocks growing in her flower pots. Extraordinarily, they were in bloom not only from spring to summer but remained in flower into the autumn and even into the winter...

Mabel's life was hidden. Like those hidden lilies, but so much more, her life glorified God. It is so often out of the limelight of public life and even of visible church life that God is glorified. The value of our lives and ministries to God will likely bear little resemblance to their estimation in the marketplace. Jesus makes plain that almost everything about our inner life and relationship with God must be expressed outside the public eye, whether it be our giving (Matthew 6:3), our praying (Matthew 6:5) or our fasting (Matthew 6:18). God sees us in secret…

God so often works subliminally in ways that are hidden, outside the values of the world and, when seen, surprising to the eyes of the world. In the parable of the sheep and the goats (Matthew 25:31–46), the dominant note is one of surprise. Some assumed their lives were pleasing to God; others did not dare presume such a thing. Each group was surprised by God's response, asking, 'When did we do this? When did we not do that?'

From John Stroyan, *Turned by Divine Love: Starting again with God and with others* (BRF, 2019), pp. 112–14.

Easter

Ro Willoughby

When I am leading Easter workshops in primary schools, we heap coats and large paper leaves on to a 'roadway' into Jerusalem; we wash feet with a bit of disgust; and we wince at the thought of nails hammered into ankle bones. All the time, we explore what emotions were flying around.

As Jesus is buried behind a hula-hoop 'stone', on the Friday evening, we solemnly pause. I ask the children how Jesus' disciples would have been feeling. Overwhelmingly sad? Scared that they too might be arrested? Disappointed that the man they'd hoped would rescue them had failed? We take a vote with a show of hands. Sadness and fear usually win. The children are always caught up in the deep, heartfelt emotions of the Easter story.

That's why I'd like to invite you to join with me in exploring the feelings that abound in the Easter story as Luke records them in his gospel. The emotions tumble over each other, but like the children in the school workshops, we also can get involved, and Christ can speak to us through these stories. For Jesus comes to stand with us and declares, 'Peace be with you!', as he did on that first Easter day. You will likely be familiar with the stories, but I pray that God by his Spirit will bring you a fresh experience of himself as you read them again.

Luke 19:35–37 (NIV, abridged)

Feeling excited

[The disciples] threw their cloaks on the colt and put Jesus on it. As he went along, people spread their cloaks on the road… The whole crowd of disciples began joyfully to praise God in loud voices for all the miracles they had seen.

Dr Helen Roseveare was a missionary doctor in the Belgian Congo, now the DRC, from 1953 to 1973. At great cost, she established a medical training centre and was much loved by patients and students. Some years later, word got around that she was coming to visit. Thousands travelled for days to meet her. She was completely overwhelmed by their excited, joyful welcome. Dr Helen had returned!

For centuries, the Jews had expected their Messiah, the promised one from God, to come. Hundreds have already gathered in Jerusalem for the Passover festival. The crowds have seen the miracles Jesus has performed. They have heard him speak. The prophet Zechariah said their king would come riding on a colt. When Jesus rides into the city of Jerusalem on a donkey, there is an explosion of excitement. Here is their king!

One definition of 'excitement' is 'a feeling of deep enthusiasm and eagerness'. Unlike the Jews, we are not waiting for Christ who, by his Spirit, has already come to us. Nonetheless, our excitement and joy in him can bubble inside us.

■ PRAYER

Lord Jesus, may your presence fill me with a deep and eager enthusiasm to 'know you more clearly, love you more dearly and follow you nearly'. Amen

* St Richard of Chichester (1197–1253)

Luke 22:14–15, 19, 33–34 (NIV, abridged)

Feeling confused

*When the hour came, Jesus and his apostles reclined at the table.
And he said to them, 'I have eagerly desired to eat this Passover with
you before I suffer…' He took bread, gave thanks and broke it, and
gave it to them, saying, 'This is my body given for you…' [Peter said,]
'Lord, I am ready to go with you to prison and to death.' Jesus
answered, '… Before the cock crows today, you'll deny three times
that you know me.'*

Sometimes I'm listening to people talking, but I don't really
understand what's being talked about, although the topic sounds
familiar. I'd like to join in, but if I do, I may end up looking stupid. I'm
confused.

Jesus' disciples know his enemies are plotting Jesus' death. During
this Passover meal in Jerusalem, Jesus continues to prepare his
disciples for his imminent death. Yet how can they grasp what he's
talking about? They are confused. Peter demonstrates his confusion
by confidently and bravely declaring his loyalty.

But Jesus gives them clues that will soon lessen their confusion.
He gives them the symbols of remembrance – bread and wine. Ever
since his resurrection, Christians have the key to make some sense
of Jesus' death. In what ways does the last supper bring order and
peace to you?

■ PRAYER

*The body of our Lord Jesus Christ was broken for us to preserve our
body and soul unto everlasting life. May we eat the bread and feed on
him in our hearts by faith with thanksgiving. Amen*

Luke 22:41–44 (NIV)

Feeling afraid

[Jesus] withdrew about a stone's throw beyond [his disciples], knelt down and prayed, 'Father, if you are willing, take this cup from me; yet not my will, but yours be done.' An angel from heaven appeared to him and strengthened him. And being in anguish, he prayed more earnestly, and his sweat was like drops of blood falling to the ground.

People respond in different ways to intense fear. Two standard responses are either to take flight or prepare to fight. Jesus does neither of these. He remains in the garden of Gethsemane, knowing his enemies and officers of the temple guard will come to arrest him, leading to his excruciating death. He pleads with God to put an end to what is to come, yet he is prepared to do what his Father wants. The intensity of his fear is seen as tiny blood vessels on his face burst and blood escapes through the sweat glands. This is a rarely seen medical condition. An angel strengthens him. He does not run away, nor does he act violently.

We should not forget that Jesus' disciples are also afraid. They sleep with exhaustion and almost all of them run away.

Many things may make us afraid, but we can cry out to God, pleading for him to hear, knowing that Jesus truly understands. His Spirit comforts us.

■ **PRAYER**

Words from Psalm 23 give us confidence in God amidst our fears: 'Even though I walk through the darkest valley, I will fear no evil, for you are with me.' Amen

Luke 22:59–62 (NIV, abridged)

Feeling full of shame

About an hour later another asserted, 'Certainly this fellow was with him, for he is a Galilean.' Peter replied, 'Man, I don't know what you're talking about!' Just as he was speaking, the cock crowed. The Lord turned and looked straight at Peter. Then Peter remembered the word the Lord had spoken to him… And he went outside and wept bitterly.

Earlier on in this series, we read about Peter's boast that he would never desert Jesus. After Jesus is arrested, Peter remains close to where Jesus is. He's given three opportunities to publicly admit his relationship with Jesus, yet each time he denies him. The third time Jesus is present and catches Peter's eye. Peter remembers what Jesus said. He's let Jesus down. How ashamed he must have felt!

After the resurrection, Jesus does not refer to Peter's betrayal but commissions him for the future. We've all let someone down at some point in our lives and, most significantly, we have all failed to live up to what God requires of us. But once we know we have been forgiven by him, our shame is wiped away.

■ PRAYER

'If we claim to be without sin, we deceive ourselves and the truth is not in us. If we confess our sins, he is faithful and just and will forgive us our sins and purify us from all unrighteousness' (1 John 1:8–9). Tell God about anything that makes you ashamed. Ask for and then receive his forgiveness.

Luke 23:1–4 (NIV)

Feeling out of control

Then the whole assembly rose and led [Jesus] off to Pilate. And they began to accuse him, saying, 'We have found this man subverting our nation. He opposes payment of taxes to Caesar and claims to be Messiah, a king.' So Pilate asked Jesus, 'Are you the king of the Jews?' 'You have said so,' Jesus replied. Then Pilate announced to the chief priests and the crowd, 'I find no basis for a charge against this man.'

Occasionally I'm in a group where the person supposed to be in charge isn't in control. Someone else is in authority. At Jesus' trial, several people claimed to be in control, yet ultimately they were all powerless.

The chief priests determined to get rid of Jesus had no power to put anyone to death. They depended on the Roman authorities to act on their false accusations.

The authority of Rome rested on the shoulders of Pilate, the Roman governor. He was unconvinced that Jesus had done anything wrong, yet he was so fearful of the crowd that he wouldn't release Jesus.

The people were weak, too easily persuaded by the Jewish authorities to demand the death penalty.

The only person with real power – the one in authority who said little – was Jesus himself. He chose not to exercise his power to rescue himself. We may feel powerless, out of control or trapped by circumstances, but Christ understands powerlessness more than anyone. He is all-powerful, and we can trust him to walk with us.

■ PRAYER

Tell the almighty God about what makes you feel helpless, and ask him to reassure you.

Luke 23:44–46 (NIV)

Feeling satisfied

It was now about noon, and darkness came over the whole land until three in the afternoon, for the sun stopped shining. And the curtain of the temple was torn in two. Jesus called out with a loud voice, 'Father, into your hands I commit my spirit.' When he had said this, he breathed his last.

Have you ever planned something like a mountain-climbing expedition? You gather your fellow climbers together, assemble the necessary equipment, get started, keep persevering and reach the summit, before finally coming back to base camp. You may be utterly exhausted, but you have a right to feel satisfied. Job done.

Jesus had a growing sense of his destiny. Ultimately, he knew he'd come to die an agonising death. John records Jesus' last words on the cross, 'It is finished!' Luke writes that Jesus committed himself to his Father. Both gospels are recording the moment when Jesus accepted that he had fulfilled his mission. He'd taken the blame and guilt for the sin of the whole world. The significance of Christ's death is demonstrated symbolically by the curtain in the temple being torn from top to bottom. This had separated the most holy place from the people. Now, the way to God is freely open. There's a right sense of agony-filled satisfaction. Job done.

■ PRAYER

Reflect on the immensity of what Jesus did in dying on the cross, making it possible for all people to enter God's presence without shame. Tell God how this makes you feel.

Luke 23:52–53a, 55–56a (NIV)

Feeling full of grief

Going to Pilate, [Joseph of Arimathea] asked for Jesus' body. Then he took it down, wrapped it in linen cloth and placed it in a new tomb cut in the rock… The women who had come with Jesus from Galilee followed Joseph and saw the tomb and how his body was laid in it. Then they went home and prepared spices and perfumes.

Many people stood at the foot of the cross and watched Jesus die – the experienced Roman soldiers, Jesus' enemies, regular spectators of executions, some of Jesus' family and friends. Jesus spoke to his mother and asked his beloved disciple to look after her. And once he had given up his spirit, he died.

Those who loved him had stayed at a distance, watching. Bravely, as it got dark, Joseph of Arimathea moved decisively to get permission to bury Jesus' body in a new tomb before the sabbath began. The women would have to wait 36 hours to take their prepared spices to perfume Jesus' body. These were all people who, in their confusion and deep sorrow at Jesus' death, showed their love for him by their actions. They were not to know that Jesus had conquered death, that this was not the end.

■ **PRAYER**

Pray for anyone you know who is grieving the death of someone they love. Pray especially for those who are recently bereaved and may be coping with their sorrow by being very busy. May God comfort them in their busyness.

Luke 24:1–6a (NIV, abridged)

Feeling shocked

On the first day of the week, very early in the morning, the women…
found the stone rolled away from the tomb, but when they entered,
they did not find the body of the Lord Jesus… Suddenly two men in
clothes that gleamed like lightning stood beside them. In their fright
the women bowed down with their faces to the ground, but the men
said to them, 'Why do you look for the living among the dead? He is
not here; he has risen!'

Throughout the Bible, the first thing angels usually say is, 'Do not be afraid.' These women, bringing spices to anoint Jesus' dead body, are terrified by these gleaming angelic beings. But the angels don't acknowledge their fright; they simply ask a question and make an astounding announcement: Jesus is alive, so he won't be found in a graveyard.

We may be so familiar with the Easter story that we forget how shocking it was for Jesus' family and friends. First his body was gone and then they're told he's no longer dead. They're in for many more surprises as they encounter the risen Jesus, whose resurrection body is the same, but different. The scars are there, but his body is no longer broken. Imagine how hard it must have been for these women to absorb the message of the gleaming angels.

Our own fragile bodies will not last. But when we enter the eternal presence of Christ, our resurrection bodies will be vibrantly alive.

■ PRAYER

Lord Jesus, your resurrection body hints at what we will be like. Being
reminded of this, help me today to cope with my own aches and pains.
Amen

Luke 24:30–34 (NIV, abridged)

Feeling thrilled

When he was at the table with them, he took bread, gave thanks, broke it and began to give it to them. Then their eyes were opened and they recognised him, and he disappeared from their sight. They asked each other, 'Were not our hearts burning within us while he talked with us on the road and opened the Scriptures to us?' They got up and returned at once to Jerusalem… saying, 'It is true! The Lord has risen.'

I've often been reading the Bible and, suddenly, it is as though a light bulb has gone on in my head. *Now* I understand something fresh about God. Maybe I was listening to a preacher or reading a book or quietly reflecting on some Bible verses.

Jesus' two friends walked all the way to the village of Emmaus, seven miles from Jerusalem. The stranger who caught up with them on the road took them back into the Old Testament to help them make sense of Jesus' death and the rumours that he was alive again. It must have been the greatest Bible study ever.

But the light bulb doesn't go on until Jesus breaks the bread, and of course we don't know exactly what it was that triggered their understanding. Whatever it was, they are thrilled. Similarly, God by his Spirit enables us to grasp, and be thrilled by, fresh truths about himself as we read and reflect, worship and pray.

■ PRAYER

Thank you, Lord God, that 'your word is a lamp for my feet and a light on my path'*. Thrill my heart as I read your words of truth. Amen

---

* Psalm 119:105

Luke 24:36–37, 40–43, 45 (NIV, abridged)

Emotional overload

*Jesus himself stood among them and said, 'Peace be with you.'
They were startled, thinking they saw a ghost… He showed them
his hands and feet. And while they still did not believe it because of
joy and amazement, he asked them, 'Do you have anything here to
eat?' They gave him a piece of broiled fish, and he took it and ate it…
Then he opened their minds so they could understand the Scriptures.*

I recently went to a thanksgiving service for the life of someone in my family. It was a deeply sorrowful occasion, yet we were thankful for his life. It was a joyful celebration of who he was and his faithful ministry that had enabled God to touch many, many people's lives. Emotions collided with one another. You've probably been to similar occasions.

I was reminded of this as I read these verses. The disciples are startled, scared, overjoyed, amazed, disbelieving, mentally challenged. So many confused emotions: but we've noticed such confusion throughout this series.

What happened here is that 'Jesus himself stood among them'. Seeing the resurrected Jesus was bound to bring confusion, but beyond the confusion, he brings peace and order to their minds.

This is what Jesus wants for us, however confusing life may sometimes seem. He stands with us and shares our ordinary lives. Ask him to give you his peace and order today.

■ **PRAYER**

Jesus, stand among us in your risen power and free us from all fears and sorrows, hour by hour. Amen

Landscapes of promise

Margot and Martin Hodson

Our journey through life takes us through many different places and landscapes. Even if you have mostly lived in one place, you are likely to have had holidays in special landscapes: maybe by the sea or in the mountains. How do we respond to these unfamiliar landscapes? Are we in awe of snow-covered peaks? Do the stunning autumn colours of a maple forest cause us to wonder? Do we worry on stormy sea crossings? We can learn a lot about ourselves when the geography changes.

The Bible is full of different landscapes: mountains and deserts; hills and valleys; wilderness, forest, bush and pasture; river banks and shorelines. These are the places where the people of God lived out their faith and learned to follow him more fully. God used these different environments to teach his people different things and to draw them ever closer to him.

As we look at these biblical landscapes, we too can learn more about God and gain a new perspective on our own life journey. The landscapes are often metaphors for life-circumstances and, as we step into them in our imaginations, we can see God working through them and discover a deeper understanding of our discipleship.

Deuteronomy 26:9 (NIV)

This land

He brought us to this place and gave us this land, a land flowing with milk and honey.

The phrase 'a land flowing with milk and honey' has been taken into popular usage to mean a bounteous and wealthy land or country. Many people use the phrase to describe the United States.

In the Bible it is mentioned 20 times, and there the meaning is rather more specific. In this context milk means goat's milk, which is God telling the Israelites that they would be pastoralists on the hills and not growing crops in the valleys. Honey means bees, which were most likely to be found in the forests and wild places of the hills. One thing was certain: the land the Israelites were going to was very different to the rich, irrigated landscape of Egypt that they left behind. It would be a good land, but not the same as before.

Have you ever thought you were going to 'a land flowing with milk and honey', but when you got there found it was not quite what you expected? Maybe even now you are trying to adapt to a new situation. Or are you still searching for that land? Wherever you are and whatever your situation, ask God for his blessing.

■ **PRAYER**

Lord, thank you for placing me where I am. Show me how to make this place a land flowing with milk and honey. Amen

Psalm 96:12–13 (NIV, abridged)

Forests

Let all the trees of the forest sing for joy. Let all creation rejoice before the Lord, for he comes, he comes to judge the earth.

Springtime in woodland can seem magical. In the barrenness of winter, the forest floor is dark with mud and leaf litter, and the branches of the trees stick out like dead bones from the trunks. Then spring arrives: first green shoots emerge through the leaf litter, followed by pretty woodland flowers. Then, as the spring birdsong strengthens, the tree branches burst open with delicate spring leaves. It truly seems that they sing for joy.

Getting older can seem like the winter of life. Hobbies, health and friendships can begin to wind down. But in life as in nature, we can catch those glimpses of spring: not only snowdrops and crocuses and the lengthening days, but perhaps in holding a new baby or chatting to a young relative. These are special moments and, whatever they are and whenever they come, we should make sure we treasure them.

We might wonder why the psalmist says creation rejoices in God's coming judgement. It is because by judging the earth God will redeem and renew creation. Then all the trees of the forest will truly sing for joy and we will join the eternal song of heaven with them. Praise be!

■ PRAYER

Lord, thank you for those moments of pure joy. Help us to treasure them and keep our eyes fixed on you and the joy of your redeeming love. Amen

Mark 4:39 (NIV)

Lakes

[Jesus] got up, rebuked the wind and said to the waves, 'Quiet. Be still!' Then the wind died down and it was completely calm.

The Sea of Galilee is actually a relatively small lake, and it is possible to see across it. For much of the year it is calm, and in the summer it is hot and humid at the water's edge. But when storms do come they can be quite violent, even life-threatening. When Jesus and the disciples took a boat trip from one side of the lake to the other, they got caught in such a storm. The disciples were terrified and went to wake Jesus, who was sleeping. With just three words, 'Quiet. Be still', the storm was pacified. The disciples were amazed that Jesus was able to do this. No wonder: it showed that Jesus was not only able to heal the sick, but had complete control over all aspects of the natural world.

At various times in our lives, we will know storms and rough seas. These may be illnesses, job losses or the deaths of loved ones. Maybe that is where we are right now, but Jesus will guide us through those storms and help us readjust when we reach a place of peace again. He will be with us both in the storms and in the calm that follows.

■ **PRAYER**
Lord, we pray that you will be with us both in the difficult times and in the easier times that follow them. Amen

Exodus 16:2 (NIV)

Deserts

In the desert the whole community grumbled against Moses and Aaron.

The Israelites were looking back with nostalgia. They were migrants on a long hike through a barren landscape, where food was sparse and the going was tough. They looked back to their time in Egypt, when they remembered plenty of food but forgot the forced labour and back-breaking hours. Here they were in freedom, with a new land ahead, yet they focused on the past and grumbled.

Sometimes life can feel a bit depressing, especially when we compare how things are now with how they were in the past. We may miss an exciting and prestigious job, or we may miss the times when family were all around. Maybe now, at times, we feel useless and lonely.

God was gentle in his response to the Israelites. He understood their tiredness and desperation. The story continues with the miracle of quail and manna from heaven. The Israelites did not know what manna was and would have missed it but for Moses showing them how to gather it. When life seems drab, it's tempting to look back with sadness. But resist that temptation and look instead for the signs of manna in life today. God might have some surprises in store.

■ PRAYER

Lord, help me to see what you are doing in my life now. Help me to give thanks for good things in the past and to be confident of your loving care for me now. Amen

Psalm 23:1–2a (NIV)

Pastures

The Lord is my shepherd, I lack nothing. He makes me lie down in green pastures.

This is one of the most famous and best-loved psalms. Does it make you think of rolling English countryside, lush green grass, fluffy white sheep and a border collie sheepdog with a shepherd following behind? Of course, it was rather different in its original Middle-Eastern context.

Throughout the Bible, the theme of sheep and shepherds is a strong one. This verse from Psalm 23 tells us three truths that recur again and again:

First, if we follow God we will lack nothing. This doesn't mean that we will always have all the material possessions that we want, but that we will have the spiritual resources to deal with any eventuality.

Second, we will 'lie down in green pastures', implying that the shepherd will find the perfect place for us. Again, we might not think it is the perfect place, but the shepherd always knows what is best for us.

But who is the shepherd? Jesus said of himself, 'I am the good shepherd. The good shepherd lays down his life for the sheep' (John 10:11). So, third, we can be assured that Jesus is the good shepherd and that he will look after us. All we need to do is to trust in him.

■ PRAYER
Lord, I thank you that you are the good shepherd. Show me how to be a good sheep. Amen

Jonah 2:2 (NIV)

The sea

'In my distress I called to the Lord, and he answered me. From deep in the realm of the dead I called for help, and you listened to my cry.'

It was just before Christmas. We'd both been out for the day and came home feeling lousy. Before we knew it, we were in bed experiencing the worst flu that we'd ever known. Being in a vicarage, this had some special challenges in terms of progressively finding others to cover all the Christmas services, but also some amazing blessings, with food appearing on the doorstep and many other kindnesses. We truly have a wonderful team.

We never know when the storms of life will hit us, and our flu was very minor compared to life's fiercer storms, such as life-changing illness, tragedy and bereavement. We can feel lost and abandoned by God at these times.

Jonah had been going his own way in life when tragedy hit, and he might easily have thought that all was lost. But instead, he turned to prayer.

We won't all have the miraculous rescue that Jonah had, but we can all trust in God, who cares for us and brings us salvation. When we're in a difficult situation and pray, something changes. Sometimes the situation changes, but even if it doesn't, something inside us changes so we begin to see the situation differently. We might want to pray for ourselves or for someone else. Whoever our prayer is for, we can trust God.

■ PRAYER

Lord, help us to pray in all of life's circumstances. Show us your perspective and help us to trust you more. Amen

Isaiah 35:1–2a (NIV)

Wilderness

The desert and the parched land will be glad; the wilderness will rejoice and blossom. Like the crocus, it will burst into bloom; it will rejoice greatly and shout for joy.

A friend once went camping in the dry and rocky Negev desert in Israel, during a period of rain. One morning, he woke to find that he was surrounded by a carpet of flowers. It was stunningly beautiful and he dared not move in case he trod on the flowers. Desert flower seeds can lie dormant in the ground for many years, leaving the landscape looking completely barren, but as soon as it rains the seeds germinate and the flowers bloom.

Sometimes we have gifts and talents that can lie dormant, especially through the busy years when juggling work and family takes up all our time. For some, retirement can look like a barren landscape, but this is when more spare time can be like gentle rain on the seeds of half-forgotten talents and interests, allowing them to flourish once again, or even for the first time.

Gifts and talents can be discovered – or rediscovered – and shared, bringing new vibrancy and colour to life in retirement. It's also a good time to refresh your relationship with God. If he can bring flowers to the desert, there is no telling what he can do in our lives.

■ PRAYER

Thank you, Lord, for the gift of time. Show me how to use this precious gift and lead me more deeply into your presence. Amen

Psalm 137:1 (NIV)

Rivers

By the rivers of Babylon we sat and wept when we remembered Zion.

The song 'Rivers of Babylon' was popularised by the group Boney M. in the 1970s and is one of the few pop songs to use words from the Bible. The passage from Psalm 137 refers to when the Jewish people were taken into exile in Babylon. It was a time of deep national trauma and reflection, and we can imagine the Israelites sitting on the banks of the Tigris and Euphrates rivers, looking back on the time they were in Judah and regretting all the things they had done wrong. They had ignored the warnings of their prophets and had paid the price. Now, they found themselves in captivity and in the unfamiliar land of Babylon. Inevitably, the tears came.

Hopefully, none of us will ever be in a situation as serious as the Babylonian exile. But it is quite possible that we find ourselves in unfamiliar surroundings today, or will do in the future. How do we react? A sense of loss and longing is surely only natural, but perhaps we shouldn't put all of the focus on ourselves.

There are now millions of refugees living in temporary accommodation in unfamiliar landscapes around the world. Many will have very similar feelings to the Israelites in Babylon. Let's remember them now.

■ PRAYER
Loving God, be with all those who have moved home recently, whether by choice or out of necessity. Comfort, protect and encourage them in their new surroundings. Amen

Mark 9:2 (NIV)

Mountains

Jesus took Peter, James and John with him and led them up a high mountain, where they were all alone. There he was transfigured before them.

We often hear people talking about 'mountaintop experiences': those special times with God. Peter, James and John certainly had one of those moments. As Jesus led them up Mount Hermon, his garments shone brightly, and suddenly Moses and Elijah appeared from nowhere. Then a voice from a cloud said, 'This is my Son, whom I love. Listen to him!' before things returned to normal. This was not at all a typical hike up a mountain.

But what happened next? Mark's gospel tells us that Jesus led the three disciples down the mountain, and he was soon back among the people, healing a boy who had an impure spirit. So the mountaintop experience didn't last forever, and they were soon back to work.

And so it is for us. We love, even crave, those experiences at the top of the mountain, but they're not a permanent state. God intends that we should all benefit from these experiences, but that we should then come down from the mountain to do his work. The mountaintop is where we hear and see God, but the valleys are where we live out our lives, serving God in the day-to-day.

■ **PRAYER**
Lord, if it is your will, give us a mountaintop experience. But also show us how to live in the valley below. Amen

Deuteronomy 20:19 (NIV, abridged)

Caring for the land

When you lay siege to a city for a long time… do not destroy its trees by putting an axe to them, because you can eat their fruit… Are the trees people, that you should besiege them?

Is it worth sacrificing everything to win? As a young person, it can seem so, and over time sacrifices might be regained. With maturity, we realise that few prizes are worth destroying everything else for and, ultimately, family, friends and community are those things of greatest value.

Sometimes armies have destroyed farms, woodland and orchards in battle, only to discover the cost of their loss after victory. This passage looks at the specific issue of armies cutting down orchards, but has a wider application for our care of nature as a whole. It can be seen in two ways: first, we should care for creation because we depend on it for life. If we destroy our planet, we destroy ourselves. But second, we should care for nature because it is an innocent bystander in the drama of human activity. It does not lay siege to us and so we should protect it.

In the end, we have to ask whether the goal of continuing economic growth is worth the cost of damaging God's earth beyond immediate repair. As people with the wisdom of age, we have something important to contribute in this debate.

■ PRAYER

Dear Lord, help us to value your creation and care for it more effectively. Amen

Making an impact

If someone asked you who throughout history (excluding Jesus) has left the biggest impact, what would be your answer?

For some, it may be Albert Einstein, who is responsible for developing the theory of relativity, came up with the formula $E = mc^2$ and in 1921 received the Nobel Prize in Physics.

For those who love to read, it may be someone like Johannes Gutenberg who, in 1439, invented the printing press.

Or maybe the person who has left the biggest impact, in your opinion, is someone who is close to you, whose name isn't widely known but whose contribution to your life is valuable.

Here at BRF, we have many people who contribute in such a way. They are people whose names are not widely known, but to us they are heroes.

It is because of these heroes – their willingness to partner with us and their financial gift – that we can continue inspiring and equipping future generations to grow in faith. Through access to our notes, books and creative programmes, people are encountering Jesus and lives are being impacted.

If you would like to partner with us, and the time is ever right for you to remember a charity in your will, please remember BRF.

For further information about making a gift to BRF
in your will, please visit **brf.org.uk/lastingdifference**,
contact **+44 (0)1865 319700** or email **giving@brf.org.uk**.

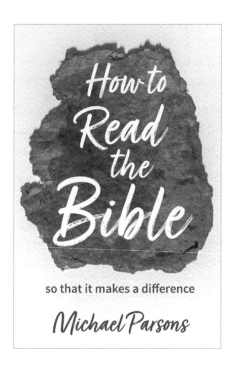

To read and engage with the Bible, we first need to understand the story, the styles of writing and the approaches we find in the text. Michael Parsons encourages readers to look at the whole biblical storyline before demonstrating ways of approaching individual texts. Topics along the way include understanding different genres, the importance of narrative, imaginative reading, praying the Bible, difficult passages and what to do with them, and how to apply scripture to our own lives.

How to Read the Bible
So that it makes a difference
Michael Parsons
978 0 85746 809 3 £8.99
brfonline.org.uk

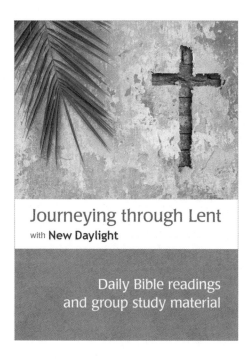

Journeying through Lent

with **New Daylight**

Daily Bible readings
and group study material

This resource provides Lent material at an affordable price, using material by well-loved contributors from the *New Daylight* archive alongside specially written questions for group discussion. It encourages groups and individuals, whether existing readers of *New Daylight* or those who are new to using Bible reading notes, to share their experience and reflect together on the Lent journey as a church community. With contributions from Helen Julian CSF, Rachel Boulding, Stephen Cottrell, Tony Horsfall and Brother Ramon SSF.

Journeying through Lent with New Daylight
Daily Bible readings and group study material
978 0 85746 965 6 £2.99
brfonline.org.uk

To order

Online: **brfonline.org.uk**
Telephone: +44 (0)1865 319700
Mon–Fri 9.15–17.30
Post: complete this form and send to the address below

Delivery times within the UK are normally 15 working days. Prices are correct at the time of going to press but may change without prior notice.

Title	Issue*	Price	Qty	Total
Turned by Divine Love		£9.99		
How to Read the Bible		£8.99		
Journeying through Lent with New Daylight		£2.99		
Bible Reflections for Older People (single copy)	May/Sep* 20	£5.15		

delete as appropriate

POSTAGE AND PACKING CHARGES			
Order value	UK	Europe	Rest of world
Under £7.00	£2.00	Available on request	
£7.00–£29.99	£3.00	Available on request	
£30.00 and over	FREE	Available on request	

Total value of books	
Postage and packing	
Total for this order	

Please complete in BLOCK CAPITALS

Title .... First name/initials .... Surname..

Address ....

.... Postcode ....

Acc. No. .... Telephone ....

Email ....

Method of payment

☐ Cheque (made payable to BRF) ☐ MasterCard / Visa

Card no. ☐☐☐☐ ☐☐☐☐ ☐☐☐☐ ☐☐☐☐

Expires end ☐☐ ☐☐ Security code* ☐☐☐ Last 3 digits on the reverse of the card

Signature* .... Date .... /............ /............

*ESSENTIAL IN ORDER TO PROCESS YOUR ORDER

Please return this form to:

BRF, 15 The Chambers, Vineyard, Abingdon OX14 3FE | enquiries@brf.org.uk
To read our terms and conditions, please visit **brfonline.org.uk/terms**.

BROP0120

The Bible Reading Fellowship (BRF) is a Registered Charity (233280)

BIBLE REFLECTIONS FOR OLDER PEOPLE GROUP SUBSCRIPTION FORM

All our Bible reading notes can be ordered online
by visiting **brfonline.org.uk/collections/subscriptions**

The group subscription rate for *Bible Reflections for Older People* will be £15.45 per person until April 2021.

☐ I would like to take out a group subscription for .... (*quantity*) copies.

☐ Please start my order with the May 2020 / September 2020 / January 2021* issue.
I would like to pay annually/receive an invoice with each edition of the notes.* (*delete as appropriate*)

Please do not send any money with your order. Send your order to BRF and we will send you an invoice. The group subscription year is from 1 May to 30 April. If you start subscribing in the middle of a subscription year we will invoice you for the remaining number of issues left in that year.

Name and address of the person organising the group subscription:

Title .... First name/initials .... Surname...

Address..

.... Postcode ....

Telephone... Email...

Church...

Name of minister ....

Name and address of the person paying the invoice if the invoice needs to be sent directly to them:

Title .... First name/initials .... Surname...

Address..

.... Postcode ....

Telephone... Email...

Please return this form to:
BRF, 15 The Chambers, Vineyard, Abingdon OX14 3FE | enquiries@brf.org.uk
To read our terms and conditions, please visit **brfonline.org.uk/terms**.

BROP0120   The Bible Reading Fellowship is a Registered Charity (233280)

BIBLE REFLECTIONS FOR OLDER PEOPLE INDIVIDUAL/GIFT SUBSCRIPTION FORM

> To order online, please visit **brfonline.org.uk/collections/subscriptions**

☐ I would like to take out a subscription (*complete your name and address details only once*)
☐ I would like to give a gift subscription (*please provide both names and addresses*)

Title .... First name/initials .... Surname ....

Address ....

.... Postcode ....

Telephone .... Email ....

Gift subscription name ....

Gift subscription address ....

.... Postcode ....

Gift message (*20 words max. or include your own gift card*):

....

....

Please send *Bible Reflections for Older People* beginning with the May 2020 / September 2020 / January 2021* issue (*delete as appropriate*):

(*please tick box*)	UK	Europe	Rest of world
Bible Reflections for Older People	☐ £19.65	☐ £27.30	☐ £31.35

Total enclosed £ .... (*cheques should be made payable to 'BRF'*)

Please charge my MasterCard / Visa ☐ Debit card ☐ with £ ....

Card no. ☐☐☐☐ ☐☐☐☐ ☐☐☐☐ ☐☐☐☐

Expires end ☐☐☐☐   Security code* ☐☐☐   Last 3 digits on the reverse of the card

Signature* .... Date ..../......./.......

*ESSENTIAL IN ORDER TO PROCESS YOUR ORDER

Please return this form to:
BRF, 15 The Chambers, Vineyard, Abingdon OX14 3FE | enquiries@brf.org.uk
To read our terms and conditions, please visit **brfonline.org.uk/terms**.

BROP0120   The Bible Reading Fellowship is a Registered Charity (233280)